SO-BZA-521

INTERBEING

Other Books by Thich Nhat Hanh

Being Peace

The Blooming of a Lotus:
Guided Meditation Exercises for Healing and Transformation

Breathe! You Are Alive: Sutra on the Full Awareness of Breathing

Call Me by My True Names: The Collected Poems of Thich Nhat Hanh

The Diamond That Cuts through Illusion:
Commentaries on the Prajñaparamita Diamond Sutra

For a Future to Be Possible:
Commentaries on the Five Wonderful Precepts

A Guide to Walking Meditation

The Heart of Understanding:
Commentaries on the Prajñaparamita Heart Sutra

Hermitage among the Clouds

Love in Action: Writings on Nonviolent Social Change

The Miracle of Mindfulness: A Manual on Meditation

The Moon Bamboo

Old Path White Clouds: Walking in the Footsteps of the Buddha

Our Appointment With Life: Buddha's Teaching on Living in the Present
(Sutra on Knowing the Better Way to Live Alone)

Peace Is Every Step: The Path of Mindfulness in Everyday Life

Present Moment Wonderful Moment: Mindfulness Verses for Daily Living

The Sun My Heart: From Mindfulness to Insight Contemplation

A Taste of Earth and Other Legends of Vietnam

Thundering Silence: Sutra on Knowing the Better Way to Catch a Snake

Touching Peace: Practicing the Art of Mindful Living

Transformation and Healing:
Sutra on the Four Establishments of Mindfulness

INTERBEING

*Fourteen Guidelines
for Engaged Buddhism*

Thich Nhat Hanh

revised edition
edited by Fred Eppsteiner

Parallax Press
Berkeley, California

Parallax Press
P.O. Box 7355
Berkeley, CA 94707

© 1987, by Thich Nhat Hanh
Revised edition © 1993, by Thich Nhat Hanh

All Rights Reserved
Printed in the United States of America
Design by Ayelet Maida
Art and calligraphy by Kazuaki Tanahashi

LIBRARY OF CONGRESS CATALOGING-IN-PUBLICATION DATA

Nhât Hanh, Thích.
    Interbeing : fourteen guidelines for engaged Buddhism
/ Thich Nhat Hanh : edited by Fred Eppsteiner. — Rev. ed.
        p. cm.
    ISBN 0-938077-59-7 (pbk.) : $8.00
    1. Tiep Hien (Religious order)   2. Buddhist precepts.
I. Eppsteiner, Fred.
BQ9800.T5392N4545   1993
294.3'65 — dc20   93-31452
                                                    CIP

Contents

PART ONE
The Order of Interbeing

PART TWO
Commentaries on the Fourteen Precepts

Editor's Introduction

The Order of Interbeing (*Tiep Hien*) was formed by Thich Nhat Hanh in the mid-1960s, at a time when the Vietnam War was escalating and the teachings of the Buddha were desperately needed to combat the hatred, violence, and divisiveness enveloping his country. On the full moon day of February 1966, Zen Master Nhat Hanh ordained six members into the Order, three men and three women ranging in age from twenty-two to thirty-two. All of them were Board members of the School of Youth for Social Service, which he had helped found the year before.

From its inception, the Order of Interbeing was comprised of all four membership categories of the original Buddhist community (*sangha*)—monks, nuns, laymen, and laywomen. Of the first six ordainees, the three women chose to live celibate lives like nuns, although they did not shave their heads or take all the formal vows of Buddhist nuns, and the three men chose to marry and practice as lay Buddhists.

The ordination was a wonderful celebration. Each ordainee was presented with a lamp with a handmade shade on which Thich Nhat Hanh had calligraphed Chinese characters like "Lamp of Wisdom," "Lamp of the Full Moon," and "Lamp of the World." During the ceremony, the six ordainees vowed to study, practice, and observe the Fourteen Precepts of the Order of Interbeing, a wonderful blend of traditional Buddhist morality and contemporary social concerns.

Forged in the crucible of war and devastation, these guidelines helped the first six brothers and sisters develop serenity and learn to look more deeply into things, even during the tragedy of war. Though they continued to stay busy helping war victims, organizing demonstrations, printing books and leaflets, running social service projects, and organizing an underground for draft resisters, they renewed themselves with a Day of Mindfulness each weekend. "I so looked forward to these days," recalls Sister Chân Không. "I dwelled mindfully on each act, beginning as I placed down my overnight bag in my room, boiled water to prepare a bath, and then put on my meditation clothes. First I did walking meditation alone in the woods and picked some wildflowers and bamboo branches for flower arrangements. Then, after a few hours of dwelling mindfully in each act and releasing most of my worries, I began to feel renewed." After practicing sitting and walking meditation, the six members gathered together to recite the Fourteen Precepts and chant the *Heart of the Prajñaparamita Sutra*.

For ten years, no new members were permitted to join the Order's core community. In fact, this "period of experimentation" was extended until 1981, when Nguyen Anh Huong, a microbiologist and lay meditation teacher, became the seventh member of the Order. Today, just twelve years later, there are more than 150 members of the core community and thousands of others worldwide who regularly recite the Fourteen Precepts. *The Mindfulness Bell* newsletter lists more than 100 sanghas, groups of people in a local community who study, practice, and discuss the Fourteen Precepts. In June 1992, the Order of Interbeing held its first International Council at Plum Village, Thich Nhat Hanh's meditation retreat center in southwestern France, and the organization is continuing to take shape as a true expression of the bodhisattva practice of socially engaged Buddhism. This revised edition of the book *Interbeing* includes updates to two of the precepts—the sixth and seventh—some new commentaries, and the full text of the Order's Charter.

The Fourteen Precepts of the Order of Interbeing remain uniquely applicable to contemporary moral dilemmas. The Order was formed at a time when destruction in the name of supposedly irreconcilable "isms" was painfully evident in Vietnam. Thich Nhat Hanh was acutely aware of the need for all people to overcome ideological divisiveness, and, accordingly, the first three precepts directly reject fanaticism and political or religious self-righteousness. The fourth precept goes to the heart of Buddhist compassion and directs a challenge to all practitioners: contemplative reflection on the suffering of living beings is not enough; we must help diminish suffering through compassionate involvement. This precept suggests the lotus flower grows most beautifully when planted deep in the mud.

The fifth precept shows how Right Livelihood has implications beyond simply avoiding harmful professions; that the manner in which we spend our time, energy, and material resources is as much a moral concern as a practical one. The sixth precept extends the traditional Buddhist precept concerning anger and directs us to apply an antidote as soon as anger arises, realizing that individual anger has far-reaching social effects. The seventh precept, at the core of all of the precepts, shows us how mindfulness, awareness, and returning to the breath are the keys to maintaining ourselves in the midst of activity.

The eighth and ninth precepts address factionalism: communities rent by political, social, and religious division, issues as pressing today as in the war-torn environment in which they were forged. They provide a model of Right Speech and Right Action, never losing sight of the need to speak out about social injustice and oppression with the all-embracing, nonpartisan viewpoint of the Dharma. The traditional Buddhist precept against killing is expanded in the twelfth precept, which enjoins us to not only not destroy life, but to actively protect it. And does not the thirteenth precept on non-stealing speak to the fact that the well-stocked shelves of one country relate directly to the empty shelves of another, that profit-making at the cost of human suffering and the suffering of other living beings is immoral?

The final precept deals with sexuality, and reminds us that respecting life and committing ourselves to ending suffering is as real an issue within the most intimate of human relationships as in the political and social arenas.

The Fourteen Precepts of the Order of Interbeing are guidelines for anyone wishing to live mindfully. By developing peace and serenity through ethical and conscientious living, we can help our society make the transition from one based on greed and consumerism to one in which thoughtfulness and compassionate action are of the deepest value. The Order of Interbeing makes real what is implicit in Buddhism and all the world's great religious traditions: that compassionate living, engaged in society, is most effective if based on the techniques for centering the self and the appreciation of the sacredness of all things great and small. The teachings and practice of Buddhism engaged in society can help us all.

Fred Eppsteiner
Naples, Florida
June 1993

PART ONE

The Order of Interbeing
(Tiep Hien)

The Order of Interbeing

1
THE MEANING OF *TIEP HIEN*

The word *tiep* means "being in touch with" and "continuing." *Hien* means "realizing" and "making it here and now." For us to better understand the spirit of the Tiep Hien Order, it is helpful to begin by examining these four expressions.

What are we to be in touch with? The answer is reality, the reality of the world and the reality of the mind. To be in touch with the mind means to be aware of the processes of our inner life—feelings, perceptions, mental formations—and also to rediscover our true mind, which is the wellspring of understanding and compassion. Getting in touch with true mind is like digging deep in the soil and reaching a hidden source that fills our well with fresh water. When we discover our true mind, we are filled with understanding and compassion, which nourishes us and those around us as well. Being in touch with the true mind is being in touch with *buddhas* and *bodhisattvas*, enlightened beings who show us the way of understanding, peace, and happiness.

To be in touch with the reality of the world means to be in touch with everything that is around us in the animal, vegetal, and mineral realms. If we want to be in touch, we have to get out of our shell and look clearly and deeply at the wonders of life—the snowflakes, the moonlight, the songs of the birds, the beautiful flowers—and also the suffering—

4 THICH NHAT HANH

hunger, disease, torture, and oppression. Overflowing with understanding and compassion, we can appreciate the wonders of life, and, at the same time, act with the firm resolve to alleviate the suffering. Too many people distinguish between the inner world of our mind and the world outside, but these worlds are not separate. They belong to the same reality. The ideas of inside and outside are helpful in everyday life, but they can become an obstacle that prevents us from experiencing ultimate reality. If we look deeply into our mind, we see the world deeply at the same time. If we understand the world, we understand our mind. This is called "the unity of mind and world."

Modern Christianity uses the ideas of vertical and horizontal theology. Spiritual life is the vertical dimension of getting in touch with God, while social life is the horizontal dimension of getting in touch with humans. In Buddhism, there are people who also think in these terms. They speak about the higher level of practicing the Buddha's Way and the lower level of helping living beings. But this understanding does not accord with the true spirit of Buddhism, which teaches that buddhahood, the nature of enlightenment, is innate to every being and not just a transcendental identity. Thus, in Buddhism the vertical and horizontal are one. If we penetrate the horizontal, we find the vertical, and vice versa. This is the meaning of "being in touch with."

Next we come to the concept of continuation. Tiep means to tie two strings together to make a longer string. It means extending and perpetuating the career of enlightenment that was started and nourished by the buddhas and bodhisattvas who preceded us. It is helpful to remember that the word "buddha" means a person who is awake. The word "bodhisattva" also signifies an enlightened person. The way of enlightenment that was started by the buddhas and bodhisattvas should be continued, and this is the responsibility of all of us who undertake the practice of Buddhism. Sowing the seeds of enlightenment and taking good care of the tree of enlightenment are the meaning of tiep, "to continue."

The third concept is "to realize" or realization. Hien means not to dwell or be caught in the world of doctrines and ideas, but to bring and express our insights into real life. Ideas about understanding and compassion are not understanding and compassion. Understanding and compassion must be real in our lives. They must be seen and touched. The real presence of understanding and compassion will alleviate suffering and cause joy to be born. But to realize does not only mean to act. First of all, realization means transforming ourselves. This transformation creates a harmony between ourselves and nature, between our own joy and the joy of others. Once we get in touch with the source of understanding and compassion, this transformation is realized and all our actions will naturally protect and enhance life. If we wish to share joy and happiness with others, we must have joy and happiness within ourselves. If we wish to share calmness and serenity, we should first realize them within ourselves. Without a calm and peaceful mind, our actions will only create more trouble and destruction in the world.

The last expression to examine is "making it here and now." Only the present moment is real and available to us. The peace we desire is not in some distant future, but it is something we can realize in the present moment. To practice Buddhism does not mean to endure hardship now for the sake of peace and liberation in the future. The purpose of practice is not to be reborn in some paradise or buddha-land after death. The purpose is to have peace for ourselves and others right now, while we are alive and breathing. Means and ends cannot be separated. Bodhisattvas are careful about causes, while ordinary people care more about effects, because bodhisattvas see that cause and effect are one. Means are ends in themselves. An enlightened person never says, "This is only a means." Based on the insight that means *are* ends, all activities and practices should be entered into mindfully and peacefully. While sitting, walking, cleaning, working, or serving, we should feel peace within ourselves. The aim of sitting meditation is first to be peaceful and awake during sitting meditation. Working to help the hungry or the sick means to be peaceful and loving during that work. When we practice, we do not expect the practice to pay large rewards in the future, even nirvana, the pure land, enlightenment, or buddhahood. The secret of Buddhism is to be awake here and now. There is no way to peace; peace is the way. There is no way to enlightenment; enlightenment is the way. There is no way to liberation; liberation is the way.

Thus far, we have examined the meanings of the words "tiep" and "hien." In looking for an English word or phrase to express the meaning of Tiep Hien, the word "interbeing" has been proposed. It is a translation of a Chinese term found in the teaching of the *Avatamsaka Sutra*. I hope this recently invented word will be widely adopted in the near future.

2
BUDDHIST PRECEPTS

Members of the Order of Interbeing observe fourteen precepts. The Sanskrit word *sila* means precept as an intention of mind that manifests in body and speech. Buddhist precepts are not prohibitions. They are guidelines for living mindfully. The practice of precepts does not restrict our liberty. On the contrary, the practice of precepts protects us and guarantees our liberty and prevents us from getting entangled in difficulties and confusion. The word "precept" should be understood in terms of the Threefold Training: *sila, samadhi*, and *prajña*, or precepts, concentration, and insight. Precepts lead to concentration, and concentration leads to insight. Thus, precepts are fundamentally disciplines of the mind, or mindfulness.

But, we should also understand the interbeing of the Threefold Training. Precepts lead to concentration and insight, and they themselves are concentration and insight. The same is true, at the same time, of concentration and insight. Perhaps the most appropriate definition of sila is "the practice of being awake, or mindful, during each bodily, verbal, and mental activity." It is only within this broad definition that the precepts can embrace and engender concentration and wisdom. Following the traditional commandments not to kill, not to steal, not to commit adultery, not to lie, and not to drink alcohol will bring about safety, joy, and peace, but is not enough to produce concentration and insight. In the context of practicing the Fourteen Precepts of the Order of Interbeing, the word "precept" fully embraces in itself the meaning of awakening. If we truly observe the precepts of the Order of Interbeing in our daily lives, we cultivate concentration and insight at the same time.

3
THE CHARTER OF THE ORDER OF INTERBEING

According to the Charter of the Order of Interbeing, "the aim of the Order is to actualize Buddhism by studying, experimenting with, and applying Buddhism in modern life." Understanding can only be attained through direct experience. The results of the practice should be tangible and verifiable.

The Charter lists four principles as the foundation of the Order: nonattachment from views, direct experimentation on the nature of interdependent origination through meditation, appropriateness, and skillful means. Let us examine each of these principles.

1. Nonattachment from views: To be attached means to be caught in dogmas, prejudices, habits, and what we consider to be the Truth. The first aim of the practice is to be free of all attachments, especially attachments to views. This is the most important teaching of Buddhism.

2. Direct experimentation: Buddhism emphasizes the direct experience of reality, not speculative philosophy. Direct practice-realization, not intellectual research, brings about insight. Our own life is the instrument through which we experiment with truth.

3. Appropriateness: A teaching, in order to bring about understanding and compassion, must reflect the needs of people and the realities of society. To do this, it must meet two criteria: it must conform with the basic tenets of Bud-

dhism, and it must be truly helpful and relevant. It is said that there are 84,000 Dharma doors through which one can enter Buddhism. For Buddhism to continue as a living source of wisdom and peace, even more doors should be opened.

4. Skillful means (*upaya*): Skillful means consist of images and methods created by intelligent teachers to show the Buddha's way and guide people in their efforts to practice the way in their own particular circumstances. These means are called Dharma doors.

Concerning these four principles, the Charter says, "The spirit of nonattachment from views and the spirit of direct experimentation lead to open-mindedness and compassion, both in the realm of the perception of reality and in the realm of human relationships. The spirit of appropriateness and the spirit of skillful means lead to a capacity to be creative and to reconcile, both of which are necessary for the service of living beings." Guided by these principles, the Order of Interbeing has an open attitude towards all Buddhist schools. The Order of Interbeing does not consider any sutra or group of sutras as its basic text. Inspiration is drawn from the essence of the Buddhadharma as found in all sutras. The Order does not recognize any systematic arrangement of the Buddhist teachings as proposed by various schools of Buddhism. The Order seeks to realize the Dharma spirit within early Buddhism as well as the development of that spirit throughout the sangha's history and the teachings in all Buddhist traditions.

In addition, the Charter expresses a willingness to be open and to change. "The Order of Interbeing rejects dogmatism in both looking and acting. It seeks all forms of action that can revive and sustain the true spirit of insight and compassion in life. It considers this spirit to be more important than any Buddhist institution or tradition. With the aspiration of a bodhisattva, members of the Order of Interbeing seek to change themselves in order to change society in the direction of compassion and understanding by living a joyful and mindful life."

4
THE COMMUNITY

The Order of Interbeing consists of a core community and an extended community. The core community is composed of members who have taken the vows to observe the Fourteen Precepts of the Order. The extended community consists of those who attempt to live up to the spirit of the Order, but who have not formally taken the vows. Members of the extended community cooperate closely with core community members in all activities. They also participate in the recitation of the Fourteen Precepts. In order to become a member of the core community, a person undergoes a one-year apprenticeship, practicing with members of a core community. After ordination, he or she agrees to observe at least sixty days of mindfulness a year.

5
THE PRECEPTS OF THE ORDER OF INTERBEING

Buddhist precepts are not sets of rules. They are guidelines for everyday living. Most religious rules are prohibitions that begin with the control of bodily actions—not to kill, steal, and so forth. The Fourteen Precepts of the Order of Interbeing begin with the mind, and the first seven precepts deal with problems associated with the mind. According to the Buddha, "The mind is the king of all dharmas. The mind is the painter who paints everything." The Fourteen Precepts reflect very truly the Eightfold Path, the basic teaching of both Theravada and Mahayana Buddhism. The Eightfold Path can be described as the essential precept (Pali: *paññatti-sila*). The Eightfold Path also begins with the mind—Right View and Right Thought. We can arrange the Fourteen Precepts into three categories. The first seven deal with the mind, the next two with speech, and the last five with the body, although we must realize that this division is arbitrary. The mind is like a lamp of awareness, always present. Those who regularly recite and practice the precepts will see this.

6
RECITING THE PRECEPTS

The Fourteen Precepts are recited at least once every two weeks. Usually, a member of the core community is asked to lead the recitation. However, a member of the extended community can also be invited to lead. Participants sit in two rows facing each other. The person who sits at the beginning of the row on the right, nearest the altar, is called the "head of the ceremony." He or she leads the ceremony and is responsible for inviting the bell to sound. The person who sits directly opposite him or her recites the precepts. The recitation should be neither too slow nor too quick, as the right speed will please the community. As the leader of the recitation, she should be visible to everyone.

At the beginning of the recitation, the head of the ceremony offers incense and recites aloud the incense-offering verse. The rest of the community stands up and, with palms joined, follows their breathing. After the incense offering, the head of the ceremony invokes the names of Shakyamuni, Manjusri, Samantabhadra, Avalokitesvara, Maitreya, and all future teachers. After each name is invoked, everyone bows together. Then the members of the community sit down. When everyone is completely settled, the bell is invited to sound, and the recitation begins with the sutra-opening verse. From the very beginning of the ceremony and recitation, everyone follows his or her breathing and practices mindfulness in each movement. When listening, joining palms together, bowing, sitting down, or even adjusting posture, there is an appropriate verse for each movement.[1]

During the recitation, each member of the community should give full attention to the precept being read in order to receive and examine its content. Concentrating on the precepts this way will keep distracting thoughts from the mind. The person who recites the precepts should speak in a clear voice that communicates the spirit of the precepts. The community's successful concentration depends on the quality of her recitation.

She begins by asking, "Brothers and Sisters, are you ready?" and each person answers silently, "Yes." After reciting each precept, she should pause for the length of three breaths, in and out, before asking, "This is the (first) precept of the Order of Interbeing. Have you studied, practiced, and observed it during the past two weeks?" This pause allows everyone to dwell on the essence and the content of the precept. The answer to the question falls somewhere between

---

[1] See *Plum Village Chanting Book* (Berkeley: Parallax Press, 1991) for incense offering verse, invoking the bodhisattvas' names, and verses for various movements. See also *Present Moment Wonderful Moment: Mindfulness Verses for Daily Living* (Berkeley: Parallax Press, 1989).

"yes" and "no." Everyone who practices mindfulness and observes the precepts is entitled to say "yes"; it would be wrong to say "no." But our "yes" is not absolutely firm, because our efforts during the past two weeks may not have been enough. So our answer is something like, "Yes, but I could have done better." We should allow time for the question to go deep into our mind and heart and act on us during the silence of the three breaths. While allowing the question to enter us, we can follow our breathing attentively. The ceremony head should deeply observe three breaths before inviting the bell to sound, and the reciter should maintain awareness of the community's questioning. When the bell sounds, the entire community joins their palms, and the person reciting proceeds to the next precept. During this time of breathing, if anyone has a copy of the text of the ceremony, he or she should refrain from touching the page until the bell is sounded. Practicing in this way creates a serene atmosphere.

The Fourteen Precepts

1

Do not be idolatrous about or bound to any doctrine, theory, or ideology, even Buddhist ones. Buddhist systems of thought are guiding means; they are not absolute truth.

2

Do not think the knowledge you presently possess is changeless, absolute truth. Avoid being narrow-minded and bound to present views. Learn and practice nonattachment from views in order to be open to receive others' viewpoints. Truth is found in life and not merely in conceptual knowledge. Be ready to learn throughout your entire life and to observe reality in yourself and in the world at all times.

3

Do not force others, including children, by any means whatsoever, to adopt your views, whether by authority, threat, money, propaganda, or even education. However, through compassionate dialogue, help others renounce fanaticism and narrowness.

4

Do not avoid contact with suffering or close your eyes before suffering. Do not lose awareness of the existence of suffering in the life of the world. Find ways to be with those who are suffering, including personal contact, visits, images, and sounds. By such means, awaken yourself and others to the reality of suffering in the world.

5

Do not accumulate wealth while millions are hungry. Do not take as the aim of your life fame, profit, wealth, or sensual pleasure. Live simply and share time, energy, and material resources with those who are in need.

6

Do not maintain anger or hatred. Learn to penetrate and transform them when they are still seeds in your consciousness. As soon as they arise, turn your attention to your breath in order to see and understand the nature of your anger and hatred and the nature of the persons who have caused your anger and hatred.

7

Do not lose yourself in dispersion and in your surroundings. Practice mindful breathing to come back to what is happening in the present moment. Be in touch with what is wondrous, refreshing, and healing both inside and around you. Plant seeds of joy, peace, and understanding in yourself in order to facilitate the work of transformation in the depths of your consciousness.

8

Do not utter words that can create discord and cause the community to break. Make every effort to reconcile and resolve all conflicts, however small.

9

Do not say untruthful things for the sake of personal interest or to impress people. Do not utter words that cause division and hatred. Do not spread news that you do not know to be certain. Do not criticize or condemn things of which you are not sure. Always speak truthfully and constructively. Have the courage to speak out about situations of injustice, even when doing so may threaten your own safety.

10

Do not use the Buddhist community for personal gain or profit, or transform your community into a political party. A religious community, however, should take a clear stand against oppression and injustice and should strive to change the situation without engaging in partisan conflicts.

11

Do not live with a vocation that is harmful to humans and nature. Do not invest in companies that deprive others of their chance to live. Select a vocation that helps realize your ideal of compassion.

12

Do not kill. Do not let others kill. Find whatever means possible to protect life and prevent war.

13

Possess nothing that should belong to others. Respect the property of others, but prevent others from profiting from human suffering or the suffering of other species on Earth.

14

Do not mistreat your body. Learn to handle it with respect. Do not look on your body as only an instrument. Preserve vital energies (sexual, breath, spirit) for the realization of the Way. (For brothers and sisters who are not monks and nuns:) Sexual expression should not take place without love and a long-term commitment. In sexual relationships, be aware of future suffering that may be caused. To preserve the happiness of others, respect the rights and commitments of others. Be fully aware of the responsibility of bringing new lives into the world. Meditate on the world into which you are bringing new beings.

THE FIRST PRECEPT ∞ THE LION'S ROAR

Do not be idolatrous about or bound to any doctrine, theory, or ideology, even Buddhist ones. Buddhist systems of thought are guiding means; they are not absolute truth.

When we read sutras, discourses of the Buddha, we often hear the expression, "the great roar of the lion." This means the truth loudly and clearly proclaimed by the Buddha himself or one of his great disciples. The first precept of the Order of Interbeing is very much in that tradition. It is the compassionate voice of the Buddha calling to us.

The Buddha regarded his own teachings as a raft to cross the river and not as an absolute truth to be worshipped or clung to. He said this to prevent rigid dogmatism or fanaticism from taking root. Ideological inflexibility is responsible for so much of the conflict and violence in the world. Many Buddhist texts, including the *Kalama, Arittha (Sutra on Knowing the Better Way to Catch a Snake)*, and *Vajracchedika (Diamond That Cuts through Illusion)* sutras, address this important subject. According to Buddhist teachings, knowledge itself can be an obstacle to true understanding, and views can be a barrier to insight. Clinging to views can prevent us from arriving at a deeper, more profound understanding of reality. Buddhism urges us to transcend even our own knowledge if we wish to advance on the Path of Awakening. Views (*drsti*) are regarded as "obstacles to knowledge."

The first precept of the Order of Interbeing opens us to the total openness and absolute tolerance of Buddhism. Openness and tolerance are not merely ways to deal with people in daily life; they are truly gateways for the realization of the Way. According to Buddhism, if we do not continue to expand the boundaries of our understanding, we will be imprisoned by our views and unable to realize the Way.

In the *Sutra of One Hundred Parables*, the Buddha tells the story of a young merchant and his son. The merchant, a widower, loved his son dearly, but lost him due to the lack of wisdom. One day, while the man was away, his little boy was kidnapped by a gang of bandits, who razed the entire village before fleeing. When the young merchant returned home, he found the charred remains of a child near where his house had been, and in his suffering and confusion, mistook the charred remains for his own son. He cried unceasingly, arranged a cremation ceremony, and then carried the bag of ashes with him day and night, tied around his neck. A few months later, his little boy was able to escape from the bandits and find his way home. At midnight, he knocked on the door of his father's rebuilt house, but the father, thinking that some mischievous boy was ridiculing him, refused to open the door. The boy knocked and knocked, but the merchant clung to his view that his boy was dead, and eventually his son had to go away. This father who loved too much lost his son forever.

The Buddha said that when we are attached to views, even if the truth comes to our house and knocks on our door, we will refuse to let it in. To inflexibly embrace a view and regard it as fixed truth is to end the vital process of inquiry and awakening. The Buddha said that his teachings were like a raft to carry us across the river to the other shore. They are a *means* of helping people, and not an *end* to worship or fight over.

Clinging fanatically to an ideology or a doctrine not only prevents us from learning, but also creates bloody conflicts. The worst enemies of Buddhism are fanaticism and narrowness. Religious and ideological wars have marred the landscape of human history for millennia. Holy wars do not have a place in Buddhism, because killing destroys the value of Buddhism itself. The destruction of lives and moral values during the Vietnam War was very much the fruit of fanaticism and narrowness. The Order of Interbeing was born during that situation of utmost suffering, like a lotus flower arising from a sea of fire. Understood in this context, the first precept of the Order of Interbeing is the compassionate voice of the Buddha in an ocean of hatred and violence.

The first precept includes all other precepts, including the precept not to kill but to protect all life. According to Buddhism, actions arise in three domains: body, speech, and mind. We usually think that killing occurs in the domain of the body, but a fanatical mind can cause the killing of not just one, but millions of human beings. If we follow the guidance of the first precept, all weapons become useless.

If various kinds of medicine are needed to treat a variety of diseases, Buddhism also needs to propose various Dharma doors for people of differing circumstances. While these Dharma doors may differ from one another, they are all Dharma doors. In the same way, distinct ailments are treated with particular medicines, but all treatments use some kind of medicine, even if the medicine is merely water, air, or massage. The teachings and practices found in Buddhism may vary, but they all aim at liberating the mind. The Buddha said, "The water in the four oceans has only one taste, the taste of emancipation." Students of Buddhism need to view the various teachings in the same light. Openness and nonattachment from views should be guiding principles for all endeavors towards reconciliation and peace. They are also the doors leading into the world of ultimate reality and absolute freedom.

THE SECOND PRECEPT ❦ TRUTH IS FOUND IN LIFE

Do not think the knowledge you presently possess is changeless, absolute truth. Avoid being narrow-minded and bound to present views. Learn and practice nonattachment from views in order to be open to receive others' viewpoints. Truth is found in life and not merely in conceptual knowledge. Be ready to learn throughout your entire life and to observe reality in yourself and in the world at all times.

The second precept is born from the first, and deals with the mind also. This precept warns us not to get caught in our own knowledge. Knowledge may be necessary to think and to judge, and may be helpful in many parts of our daily life, but it is not the highest truth. When we contemplate a sunset, we think that the sun is above the horizon, but a scientist will tell us that the sun already set eight minutes earlier. It takes that long for us to see it. We realize that we saw only the sun of the past and not the sun of the present, that our perception was erroneous. But if we were to cling to our previous knowledge, we would lose the opportunity to advance in our understanding.

Buddhism teaches us to look at things in their nature of interbeing and dependent co-arising. When we do this, we free ourselves from a world in which each thing appears to have an individual identity. The mind that sees things in their interbeing dependent co-arising nature is called the mind of nondiscriminative understanding. This mind transcends all views. In Zen Buddhism, there is an expression describing this state of insight: "The road of speech has been blocked, the path of the mind has been cut."

"Truth is found in life and not merely in conceptual knowledge." How do we practice this? "Observe reality in yourself and in the world at all times." This is the Buddhist answer. To continually observe life is to practice according to the method of the *Sutra on the Four Establishments of Mindfulness (Satipatthana)*. The sutra teaches us how to be aware of what is going on in our body, our feelings, our mind, and the object of our mind, which is the world. The practice of mindfulness can help us develop concentration and insight, so that we can see reality as it is.

THE THIRD PRECEPT ஜ FREEDOM OF THOUGHT

Do not force others, including children, by any means whatsoever, to adopt your views, whether by authority, threat, money, propaganda, or even education. However, through compas-

sionate dialogue, help others renounce fanaticism and narrowness.

This third precept deals with the issue of freedom of thought, and therefore with the mind. Many parents break this precept without being aware of it. Respecting other peoples' viewpoints is a hallmark feature of Buddhism. The *Kalama Sutta* is one of the earliest charters for free inquiry. In it, the Buddha discusses the problem of who or what to believe in and which doctrine is the best. The Buddha says, "It is fine to have doubt. Do not believe in something just because people think highly of it, or because it has come from tradition, or because it is found in scriptures. Consider whether it goes against your judgment, whether it could cause harm, whether it is condemned by wise people, and, above all, whether put into practice it will bring about destruction and pain. Anything that you judge to be beautiful, accords with your judgment, is appreciated by wise people, and, once put into practice, will bring about joy and happiness, can be accepted and put into practice."

As a shadow follows an object, the third precept follows the second, because the attitude of openness and nonattachment from views creates respect for the freedom of others. Freedom is one of the most basic rights of human beings— of all humans and not just some. To be able to respect others' freedom, we need to free ourselves from attachment and fanaticism and help others to do the same. How can we help other people? "Through compassionate dialogue," says this precept. Compassionate dialogue is the essence of nonviolent action (*ahimsa*). Ahimsa begins with the energy of tolerance and loving kindness, which will be expressed in gentle, compassionate, intelligent speech that can move peoples' hearts. It then moves into the field of action to create moral and social pressure for people to change. Understanding and compassion must be the basis of all nonviolent actions. Actions motivated by anger or hatred cannot be described as nonviolent.

As parents, we must respect freedom of thought in our children, even if they are still very young. This will allow us to learn from our children. Each human being is unique in his or her characteristics, capacities, and preferences. We should try to be open in order to see and understand our children and refrain from merely imposing our predispositions on them. Although blossoms also belong to the tree, they are not the same as the roots, leaves, and twigs. We should allow blossoms to be blossoms, leaves to be leaves, and twigs to be twigs, so that each can realize its highest capacity for development.

THE FOURTH PRECEPT ৩ AWARENESS OF SUFFERING

Do not avoid contact with suffering or close your eyes before suffering. Do not lose awareness of the existence of suffering in the life of the world. Find ways to be with those who are suffering, including personal contact, visits, images, and sounds. By such means, awaken yourself and others to the reality of suffering in the world.

The first Dharma talk given by the Buddha was on the Four Noble Truths. This first truth is *dukkha*, the presence of suffering. This is the starting point of all Buddhist practice. If we are not aware that we are unwell, we will not know how to seek treatment, and we cannot be healed. The second truth is the cause of suffering, the third is the possibility of removing it, and the fourth tells us how to do it. These are liberating truths. But we cannot seek for the other three if we do not accept the presence of the first.

Suffering can have a therapeutic power. It can help us open our eyes. Awareness of suffering encourages us to search for its cause, to find out what is going on within us and in society. But we have to be careful. Too much suffering can destroy our capacity to love. We have to know our limits, to stay in touch with things that are dreadful in life and also things that are wonderful. If the first truth explains the presence of suffering in life, the third truth encourages us to touch life's joy and peace. When people say that Buddhism is pessimistic, it is because they are stressing the first truth and overlooking the third. Mahayana Buddhism takes great care to emphasize the third truth. Its literature is full of references to the green willow, the violet bamboo, and the full moon as manifestations of the true Dharma.

Interconnections between other beings and ourselves are intimate. When we are peaceful and happy, we will not create suffering in others. When we work to alleviate the suffering in others, we feel peaceful and happy. Practice is not just for ourselves, but for others and the whole of society. The meaning of *mahayana*, the great vehicle, is to help ourselves and others, to liberate ourselves *and* others.

Teachers who say not to pay attention to the problems of the world like hunger, war, oppression, and social injustice, who say that we should only practice, have not understood deeply enough the meaning of mahayana. Of course, we should practice counting the breath, meditation, and sutra study, but what is the purpose of doing these things? It is to be aware of what is going on in ourselves and in the world. What is going on in the world is also going on within our-selves, and vice versa. Once we see this clearly, we will not refuse to take a position or to act. When a village is being bombed and children and adults are suffering from wounds and death, can a Buddhist sit still in his unbombed temple? If he has wisdom and compassion, he will find ways to prac-tice Buddhism *while* helping other people. To practice Bud-dhism, it is said, is to see into one's own nature and become a buddha. If we cannot see what is going on around us, how can we see into our own nature? There is a relationship be-tween the nature of the self and the nature of suffering, in-justice, and war. To see into the true nature of the world's weapons is to see into our own true nature.

Staying in touch with the reality of suffering keeps us sane and nourishes the wellsprings of understanding (prajña) and compassion (*karuna*) in us. It affirms in us the will to practice the bodhisattva's way: "Living beings are number-less; I vow to help by rowing them to the other shore." If we cut ourselves off from the reality of suffering, this vow will have no meaning. When we help children see and under-stand the suffering of humans and other living beings, we nourish compassion and understanding in them. Every act—even eating a sandwich or spending money—is an oc-casion for us to practice awareness. We must practice in each moment of daily life and not just in the meditation hall.

THE FIFTH PRECEPT ℘ LIVING SIMPLY

Do not accumulate wealth while millions are hungry. Do not take as the aim of your life fame, profit, wealth, or sensual plea-

sure. Live simply and share time, energy, and material resources with those who are in need.

Like a branch growing out from the trunk of a tree, the fifth precept emerges naturally from the fourth. The aim of Buddhist life is to realize insight (prajña) and to help people (*maitrya*), and not to gain fame, power, or wealth. How can we have time to live the Buddhist ideal if we are constantly pursuing wealth or fame? If we do not live simply, we have to work all the time to pay our bills, and there is little time left for practice. The *Sutra on the Eight Realizations of the Great Beings* says, "The human mind is always searching for possessions and never feeling fulfilled. This causes impure actions ever to increase. Bodhisattvas, however, always remember the principle of having few desires. They live a simple life in peace in order to practice the Way, and consider the realization of perfect understanding as their only career."

In the context of modern society, simple living also means to remain as free as possible from the destructive momentum of social and economic pressures, to avoid modern diseases such as stress, depression, high blood pressure, and heart disease. We must resolve to oppose the type of modern life filled with pressures and anxieties that so many people now live. The only way out is to consume less, to be content with fewer possessions. We must discuss this with others who share our concern for finding better ways to live simply and happily together. Once we are able to live simply and happily, we are better able to help others. We have more time and energy to share. Sharing is difficult if you are wealthy. Bodhisattvas who practice the *paramita* of living a simple life are able to give both their time and their energy to others.

THE SIXTH PRECEPT ❦ COMPASSION IS UNDERSTANDING

Do not maintain anger or hatred. Learn to penetrate and transform them when they are still seeds in your consciousness. As soon as they arise, turn your attention to your breath in order to see and understand the nature of your anger and hatred and the nature of the persons who have caused your anger and hatred.

When anger or hatred arises, we need to prepare the ground so that understanding can arise. If we stop thinking, speaking, and acting, the space for us to see and understand will open up. So the moment we feel irritation arising, we need to breathe in and out consciously, putting the whole of our mind into our breathing. Then, with the energy of mindfulness, we can look deeply and see how the person who is making us angry may have helped us in the past, or how that person has suffered, or how we ourselves have been unskillful. It may take just a few moments for us to realize this, or it may take several days. Until we come to some understanding, it is best if we refrain from saying anything to the person towards whom we feel anger. Practicing walking meditation and conscious breathing is enough.

When we grow a lemon tree, we want it to be vigorous and beautiful. But, if it isn't vigorous and beautiful, we don't blame the tree. We observe it in order to understand why it isn't growing well. Perhaps we have not taken good care of it. We know it is funny to blame a lemon tree, but we do blame human beings when they are not growing well. Because our brothers, sisters, and children are humans, we think they should behave in certain ways. But human beings are not very different from lemon trees. If we take good care of them, they will grow properly. Blaming never helps. Only love and understanding can help people change. If we take good care of people, we will be rewarded by their pleasantness. Is this much different from the rewards we receive from our lemon tree?

If I had been born in the social conditions of a sea pirate and raised as a sea pirate, I would be a pirate now. A variety of interdependent causes has created the existence of the pirate. The responsibility is not solely his or his family's, but it is also society's. As I write these lines, hundreds of babies are being born near the Gulf of Siam. If politicians, educators, economists, and others do not do something to prevent it, many of these babies will become pirates in twenty-five years. Each of us shares some responsibility for the presence of pirates. Meditating on dependent origination and looking with compassionate eyes helps us see our duty and responsibility to suffering beings. Due to his capacity of seeing, the Bodhisattva Avalokitesvara is capable of loving and acting. The purpose of meditation is to see and to hear.

"Still seeds in your consciousness" means that the anger or hatred has not manifested. This precept advises us to use preventative medicine. We might think it is impossible to transform unconscious anger and hatred, that the time to transform them is when we are already feeling angry. But we *can* transform anger and hatred before they arise. During sitting meditation, we can shine the light of awareness on our unpleasant feelings and thus identify their roots. We can look directly at feelings we usually prefer to avoid, and just by our looking at them they will begin to transform. Then, when they rise up from our subconscious in the form of anger, they will not take us by surprise. Or we can plant seeds of love, compassion, and understanding in our daily lives, and those seeds will weaken the seeds of our anger. We do not have to wait for the anger to arise to do this work. In fact, it will be much more difficult to do it once anger has already arisen.

It may happen that we feel joyful and peaceful for one or two weeks, but this does not mean that during that time the seeds of anger are not there in our store consciousness. For example, when someone says something that hurts us, we may not react right away. But several weeks later, we might become angry at that person for some very small reason. I heard one story about a child who smeared excrement all over the walls of her living room. Her mother tried to remove the mess and did not appear to be angry at all. But then, a few days later, the little girl spilled some orange juice on the table and her mother became extremely angry. Obviously the seeds of the anger had been sown or suppressed when the child smeared the excrement. So, if we are mindful we can deal with our anger before it becomes a bomb ready to explode.

If we were not able to transform our anger when it was just a seed, when the anger begins to arise, we can still transform it by following our breathing. If we cannot transform it immediately, it is best if we leave the situation and take refuge in walking meditation. The Plum Village community has recently introduced a peace treaty, an agreement between family or community members for what to do when we get angry.[2]

"Look at other beings with the eyes of compassion" is a quote from the *Lotus Sutra*. The eyes of compassion are also the eyes of understanding. Compassion is the sweet water that springs forth from the source of understanding. To practice looking deeply is the basic medicine for anger and hatred.

THE SEVENTH PRECEPT ✌ MINDFUL & JOYFUL LIVING

Do not lose yourself in dispersion and in your surroundings. Practice mindful breathing to come back to what is happening in the present moment. Be in touch with what is wondrous, refreshing, and healing both inside and around you. Plant seeds of joy, peace, and understanding in yourself in order to facilitate the work of transformation in the depths of your consciousness.

Like the kernel of a peach, this precept is at the heart of the life of the Order of Interbeing. Whether you live at a meditation center, work in an office, live with your family, or study at a university, the practice of mindfulness is crucial. The Chinese character for mindfulness has two components: heart, or mind, and present moment. To be mindful means to be fully present in the moment—not one part of you washing the dishes while another part is wondering when the work will be finished. Mindfulness can be practiced throughout the day. Walking, sitting, standing, lying

---

[2] See *Touching Peace: Practicing the Art of Mindful Living* (Berkeley: Parallax Press, 1992).

down, working, and resting are all occasions for practice. Conscious breathing is the vehicle that brings us back to the present moment and keeps us here. The *Sutra on the Full Awareness of Breathing* and the *Sutra on the Four Establishments of Mindfulness* teach us how to be mindful in our body, our feelings, our mind, and the objects of our mind.

Mindfulness leads to concentration and wisdom. We develop concentration and wisdom along with a deep sense of joy and happiness because, as we see deeply into the nature of reality, we see how wonderful the world and the beings—animal, vegetal, and mineral—that inhabit it are. Without mindfulness, we will not be in touch with the wonderful flowers, the glorious moon, our children, our spouse, or our friends. These are all infinitely precious and rare, part of the interbeing nature of all things. Mindfulness makes life real, deep, and worth living. It helps us be in the here and now where true life can be encountered. It helps us get in touch with refreshing and healing elements within and around us. While practicing this, we plant and water the seeds of joy, peace, and understanding in us, the seeds that have the power to modify and transform the pain and afflictions in us. It is not solely by touching these afflictions directly that we can heal them. Often these afflictions and pain can be transformed just because of the presence of the positive seeds that we plant and water in our daily life by the practice of mindful living.

In the *Pali Canon*, the term *dittha dhamma sukha vihari* is often used. It means to dwell happily in the present moment, in this very life. If we are not happy and joyful in our practice, it will become weak. Joy and happiness nourish our practice and make it stronger. If our practice does not transform our life and bring us great joy, if we are not able to bring joy to others and to understand them, we are not practicing correctly. The wonders of the universe are revealed to us in the meditation on interdependence. We can see that for one thing to exist, everything else also needs to exist. "This is, because that is."

If the fifth precept deals with greed, and the sixth with anger, the seventh precept deals with forgetfulness and the lack of understanding. The precepts of the Order of Interbeing follow and support one another like a string of pearls.

THE EIGHTH PRECEPT ᵇ⁰ HARMONY IN THE COMMUNITY

Do not utter words that can create discord and cause the community to break. Make every effort to reconcile and resolve all conflicts, however small.

The eighth and ninth precepts deal with speech. The essence of the eighth is concord. Community life is possible only with concord. The Buddha prescribed Six Concords, six principles of community life: living together in one place, sharing material resources, observing the same precepts, practicing together and sharing the understanding of Dharma, reconciling differing viewpoints, and practicing kind speech to avoid all quarrels. These Six Concords have been practiced by Buddhist communities since the time of the Buddha and are still relevant. Even though the eighth precept deals with speech, it relates directly to all of the Six Concords. When the first five concords are practiced, it is easy to observe loving speech. When there is good communication regarding ideas and interests, quarrels are not likely to occur.

Loving speech is born from understanding and patience. Practicing the sixth precept, we found out that blaming does not help. Only understanding and love can bring about change. Reconciliation is an art, requiring us to understand both sides of a conflict. Not only do both sides bear partial responsibility, but even those of us who are not in the conflict bear some responsibility. If we had lived in mindfulness, we could have seen the earliest phases of the conflict beginning to arise and we could have helped avoid it. To reconcile is not to judge by standing outside of a conflict. It is to take some responsibility for the existence of the conflict and to make every effort to understand the suffering of both sides. Then we can communicate to each side the suffering experienced by the other side, and offer some resolution based on an ideal common to both sides. The purpose of reconciliation is not to save face or for self-interest, but to realize understanding and compassion. To help reconcile, we ourselves must *embody* understanding and compassion. Our awareness of the need for reconciliation and of our duty to work for it will empower us to act, and the success of our efforts will depend on the degree of our understanding and compassion, not only for the two sides, but for ourselves as well.

Every true community is a community of concord. Before a Buddhist community begins an activity like reciting the precepts, making a decision, or performing the ceremony of precept transmission, the chairperson always begins by asking, "Has the community gathered?"

"Yes, the community has gathered."

"Is there harmony in the community?"

"Yes, there is harmony in the community." If this is not the answer, the meeting cannot proceed. This practice is called *karman procedure*, established during the time of the Buddha, and has been practiced by communities of monks and nuns throughout the last twenty-five centuries.

THE NINTH PRECEPT ❦ MINDFUL SPEECH

Do not say untruthful things for the sake of personal interest or to impress people. Do not utter words that cause division and hatred. Do not spread news that you do not know to be certain. Do not criticize or condemn things of which you are not sure. Always speak truthfully and constructively. Have the courage to speak out about situations of injustice, even when doing so may threaten your own safety.

This is the second precept dealing with speech. The words are simple and clear. When we speak, we can create a world of love, trust, and happiness, or a hell. We should be very careful about what we say and how we say it. If we are in the habit of talking too much, we should practice talking less. We must become aware of what we say and the results of our speaking. Even within Buddhist temples, we often speak too much, making comments about everything. All of us have experienced how negative speech can create a hell.

During retreats, we have the opportunity to practice silence, reducing our speaking by at least ninety percent. This practice can be extremely beneficial. Not only do we learn to control our speech, but we can reflect and see ourselves, the people around us, and life more clearly. When we have the opportunity to be in silence, we can look deeply and smile at the flowers, the grass, the bushes, the trees, the birds, and our fellow human beings. You who have observed periods of complete silence know the benefits of such practice. With silence, a smile, and right speech, we develop peace within ourselves and the world around us. Right speech is free of lying, gossip, exaggeration, harsh language, and foolish babble. Right speech builds understanding and reconciliation. The ninth precept not only requires frankness from us, but courage as well. How many of us are brave enough to speak out about situations of injustice, even when doing so might threaten our own safety?

THE TENTH PRECEPT ❦ STANDING UP TO INJUSTICE

Do not use the Buddhist community for personal gain or profit, or transform your community into a political party. A religious community, however, should take a clear stand against oppression and injustice and should strive to change the situation without engaging in partisan conflicts.

Politicians often seek support from religious communities, but their aim is usually political. The purpose of a religious community is to guide people on the spiritual path. Therefore, to transform a religious community into a political party is to divert it from its true aim. Religious leaders may be tempted to support their government in exchange for the material well-being of their community. This has occurred throughout recorded history. In order to secure their government's support, religious communities often refrain from speaking out against oppression and injustices committed by their government. Allowing politicians to use your religious community to strengthen their political power is to surrender the spiritual leadership of your community.

"A religious community, however, should take a clear stand against oppression and injustice...." This should be done with a clear voice, based on the principles of the Four Noble Truths. The truth concerning the unjust situation should be fully exposed (the first truth: suffering). The various causes of injustice should be enumerated (the second truth: the causes of suffering). The purpose and desire for removing the injustices should be made obvious (the third truth: the removal of suffering). The measures for removing the injustice should be proposed (the fourth truth: the way to end suffering). Although religious communities are not political powers, they can use their influence to change society. Speaking out is the first step, proposing and supporting appropriate measures for change is the next. Most important is to transcend all partisan conflicts. The voice of caring and understanding must be distinct from the voice of ambition.

THE ELEVENTH PRECEPT ∽ RIGHT LIVELIHOOD

Do not live with a vocation that is harmful to humans and nature. Do not invest in companies that deprive others of their chance to live. Select a vocation that helps realize your ideal of compassion.

Right livelihood is a branch of the Noble Eightfold Path. It implies practicing a profession that harms neither humans nor nature, physically or morally. Practicing mindfulness at work helps us discover whether our livelihood is right or not. We live in a society where jobs are hard to find and it is difficult to practice right livelihood. Still, if it happens that our work entails harming life, we should try our best to find another job. We should not drown in forgetfulness. Our vocation can nourish our understanding and compassion, or it can erode them. Therefore, our work has much to do with our practice of the Way.

Many modern industries, even food manufacturing, are harmful to humans and nature. Most current farming practices are distant from right livelihood. The chemical poisons used by modern farmers harm the environment. Practicing right livelihood has become a difficult task for farmers. If they do not use chemical pesticides, it may be difficult to compete commercially. Not many farmers have the courage to practice organic farming. Right livelihood has ceased to be a purely personal matter. It is our collective karma.

Suppose I am a school teacher and I believe that nurturing love and understanding in children is a beautiful occupation, an example of right livelihood. I would object if someone asked me to stop teaching and become, for example, a butcher. However, if I meditate on the interrelatedness of all things, I will see that the butcher is not solely responsible for killing animals. He kills them for all of us who buy pieces of raw meat, cleanly wrapped and displayed at our local supermarket. The act of killing is a collective one. In forgetfulness, we may separate ourselves from the butcher, thinking his livelihood is wrong, while ours is right. However, if we didn't eat meat, the butcher wouldn't kill it or would kill less. This is why right livelihood is a collective matter. The livelihood of each person affects all of us, and vice versa. The butcher's children may benefit from my teaching, while my children, because they eat meat, share some responsibility for the butcher's livelihood of killing.

Millions of people make a living off the arms industry, manufacturing "conventional" and nuclear weapons. These so-called conventional weapons are sold to Third World countries, most of them underdeveloped. People in these countries need food, not guns, tanks, or bombs. The United States, Russia, France, Britain, and China are the primary suppliers of these weapons. Manufacturing and selling weapons is certainly not right livelihood, but the responsibility for this situation does not lie solely with the workers in the arms industry. All of us—politicians, economists, and consumers—share the responsibility for the death and destruction caused by these weapons. We do not see clearly enough, we do not speak out, and we do not organize enough national debates on this huge problem. If we could discuss these issues globally, solutions could be found. New jobs must be created so that we do not have to live on the profits of weapons manufacturing.

If we are able to work in a profession that helps us realize our ideal of compassion, we should be very grateful. Every day, we should help create proper jobs for ourselves and others by living correctly—simply and sanely. To awaken ourselves and others and to help ourselves and others are the essence of Mahayana Buddhism. Individual karma cannot be separated from collective karma. If you have the opportunity, please use your energy to improve both. This is the realization of the first of the Four Great Vows.

THE TWELFTH PRECEPT ❧ PROTECTING LIFE

Do not kill. Do not let others kill. Find whatever means possible to protect life and prevent war.

In every country in the world, killing human beings is condemned. The Buddhist precept of non-killing extends even further, to include all living beings. However, no one, not even a buddha or a bodhisattva, can observe this precept to perfection. When we take a small step or boil a cup of water, we kill many tiny living beings. The essence of this precept is to make every effort to respect and protect life, to continuously move in the direction of non-killing. We can try our best, even if we cannot succeed one hundred percent.

This precept is closely linked with the eleventh. Our patterns of livelihood and consuming have very much to do with the lives and security of humans and other living beings. There are many causes of war. War can be caused by fanaticism and narrowness, or by the will to gain political influence or economic power. Or it can be the exploitation of one society by another that is technologically or politically stronger. We can oppose wars once they have started, but it is better to also do our best to prevent wars from breaking out. The way to prevent war is to make peace. We accomplish this first in our daily life by combatting fanaticism and attachment to views, and working for social justice. We have to work vigorously against the political and economic ambitions of any country, including our own. If important issues like these are not debated on national and international levels, we will never be able to prevent war.

We begin by studying and observing this precept of non-killing in our daily lives, and then we can work to bring out the real issues of war and peace to the whole nation. If we do not live our daily lives mindfully, we ourselves are responsible, to some extent, for the structure of war. The amount of grain used in Western countries to make liquor and feed cattle, for example, is enormous. Professor François Peroux, director of the Institute of Applied Mathematics and Economics in Paris, has suggested that by reducing meat and alcohol consumption in the West by fifty percent, the grains that would become available would be enough to solve all hunger and malnutrition problems in the Third World. Deaths caused by automobile accidents and cardiovascular illnesses would also be reduced in the West if the consumption of liquor and meat would decrease.

Defense budgets in Western countries continue to be mammoth, even after the post-Cold War spending cuts. Studies show that if we could stop or significantly slow down the manufacture of weapons, we would have more than enough money to erase poverty, hunger, many diseases, and ignorance from the world. In our busy daily lives, do we have enough time to look deeply into this precept of non-killing? How many among us can honestly say that we are doing enough to observe this precept?

THE THIRTEENTH PRECEPT ❦ SOCIAL JUSTICE

Possess nothing that should belong to others. Respect the property of others, but prevent others from profiting from human suffering or the suffering of other species on Earth.

Bringing to our awareness the pain caused by social injustice, the thirteenth precept urges us to work for a more livable society. This precept is closely linked with the fourth precept (the awareness of suffering), the fifth precept (living simply), the eleventh precept (right livelihood), and the twelfth precept (the protection of life). In order to understand this precept deeply, we need to meditate on those four precepts.

Developing ways to prevent others from profiting from human suffering is the primary duty of legislators, politicians, and revolutionary leaders. However, each of us can also act in this direction. To some degree, we can stay close to oppressed people and help them protect their right to life and defend themselves against oppression and exploitation. The bodhisattva vows are immense, and each of us can vow to sit with the bodhisattvas on their life rafts.

THE FOURTEENTH PRECEPT ℘ THREE SOURCES OF ENERGY

Do not mistreat your body. Learn to handle it with respect. Do not look on your body as only an instrument. Preserve vital energies (sexual, breath, spirit) for the realization of the Way. (For brothers and sisters who are not monks and nuns:) Sexual expression should not take place without love and a long-term commitment. In sexual relationships, be aware of future suffering that may be caused. To preserve the happiness of others, respect the rights and commitments of others. Be fully aware of the responsibility of bringing new lives into the world. Meditate on the world into which you are bringing new beings.

According to Buddhism, human beings are composed of five aggregates: form, feelings, perceptions, mental formations, and consciousness. These five aggregates depend on each other to exist and to function. "This is, because that is. This is not, because that is not." We cannot separate human beings into two distinct parts, body and soul. The concept, "Body and mind are one," is familiar to Buddhists. After several years of ascetic practice in the forest, Shakyamuni Buddha realized that mistreating his body was a mistake, and he abandoned that practice. He saw that both indulging in sensual pleasure and mistreating his body were extremes to be avoided, that both lead to degeneration of mind and body. Thus, he adopted a middle way between the two extremes.

The fourteenth precept reflects not only the spirit of Buddhism, but also of other spiritual and medical traditions of the Orient. All of these traditions teach us to preserve the body and the three sources of energy: sexual, breath, and spirit. Sexual energy is the type of energy that we expend during sexual intercourse. Vital breath is the energy we expend when we speak too much and breathe too little. Spirit is the energy we expend when we worry too much. According to Oriental medicine, if these three sources of energy are depleted, the body will weaken and disease will appear. Then it will be more difficult to practice. In Taoism and also in the martial arts, there are practices for preserving and nourishing these three sources of energy.

When practicing conscious breathing—counting the breath or following the breath—we do not waste the vital breath energy, instead we strengthen it. Concentration and the enjoyment of meditation do not expend spirit, but strengthen it. Since celibate monks and nuns do not have sexual intercourse, it is easier for them to preserve their sexual energy. If one allows the three sources of energy to dry up, it will become impossible for him or her to practice and realize the Way.

In the Buddha's time, a typical monk was a quiet person
who practiced walking and sitting meditation both day and
night. He carried a bowl into the local villages every morn-
ing to beg for food and would give a short Dharma talk to
each layperson who donated some food. This way of life en-
abled him to preserve both vital breath and spirit. In the
time of the Buddha, the main reason for monks abstaining
from sexual activity was to preserve energy. This is a point
of commonality between Buddhism and most other Eastern
spiritual and medical traditions. During the most difficult
periods of his nonviolent struggles, Mahatma Gandhi also
practiced abstinence, and he advised his colleagues to do the
same in coping with tense, difficult situations. Strength of
spirit depends on these three sources of energy. In Viet-
namese, the word "spiritual" (*tinh thân*) is formed by com-
bining the words for sexual energy (tinh) and spirit (thân).
The material and the spiritual are no longer distinct, and the
name of each is used for the other. Those who have fasted
know that if the three sources of energy are not preserved,
you cannot fast for long. In 1966, the monk Thich Tri Quang
fasted in Vietnam for 100 days, because he knew how to preserve his three sources of energy.

A second reason that monks in the Buddha's time refrained from sexual activity was that they wanted to concen-
trate on their career of enlightenment. If a monk had a
family to support and take care of, he would have had little
time left for practice. Today many monks and priests are
continually busy, whether or not they have wives or children. Just having to take care of their temples and religious
communities, they are as busy as householders. One day the
monk Dai San complained to his friend that he was too busy,

and his friend replied, "Why don't you become a monk?" A monk is not supposed to be so busy. If he has no time to practice, there is really no reason to remain a monk.

A third reason that monks in the Buddha's time refrained from sexuality was to cut off "the chain of rebirth" (*samsara*). The first meaning of rebirth means to be reborn in our offspring, our children and grandchildren. During the time of the Buddha, much more so than in our own time, poverty and disease were the common lot for most people. This situation is reflected in the First Noble Truth, "Life is suffering." Imagine a family with too many children, all of them frail and ill. There is a permanent shortage of food, no medicine, and no means of contraception. Each year a new child is born. This is still common in many parts of our world, and both parents and children suffer. Rebirth must be understood in this context and with this background. For these people, a new birth is often not a joy, but a catastrophe. To give birth to a child is to perpetuate the cycle of hunger and disease. This is the continuation of samsara. The precept for celibacy during the time of the Buddha also aimed at preventing childbirth; it had a birth-control function.

Therefore, this precept is directly related to issues of population, hunger, and economic development. The presence of Buddhist monks in countries like Sri Lanka, Burma, Thailand, Laos, Cambodia, China, Vietnam, Korea, Tibet, Mongolia, and Japan for more than twenty centuries has contributed significantly to reducing the world's population by billions. The population explosion is one of the most serious problems of our day. Hunger leads to war and, in our times, wars are incredibly destructive. Countries that cannot control their populations cannot overcome poverty. And there is the threat of nuclear holocaust. Parents must be aware of the actual situation of the world. We should know the future into which we are sending our children, to motivate us to act and live in a way that can create a better future for ourselves and our children.

We must be clearly aware of the responsibility we bear in bringing new life into the world. The answer is not to stop having children, but to make the world a better place. The future of the Earth and our children depends on the way we live today. If we continue to exploit and destroy our ecosystems, if we allow the arms race to continue, if we do not curb the growth of the world's population, the Earth and humankind will not have a future. Each of our ways of life can be a brick for building a future of peace. The fourteenth precept is vast, and its observance is linked to all the other precepts of the Order of Interbeing. To understand and practice this precept deeply, we have to see the relationship between it and our daily meditation practice, the Four Noble Truths, and the Buddhist teaching on rebirth.

These are the Fourteen Precepts of the Order of Interbeing. If we practice these precepts deeply enough, we will recognize that each precept contains every other precept. Studying and practicing them can help us understand the true nature of interbeing—we cannot just be by ourselves alone; we can only inter-be with everyone and everything else. To practice these precepts is to become aware of what is going on in our bodies, our minds, and the world. What is going on is very important. With awareness, we can live our lives happily, fully present in each moment we are alive, intelligently seeking solutions to the problems we face, and working for peace in small and large ways. I hope you will join me in practicing these precepts or the equivalent from your own tradition. It is crucial for our own well-being and the well-being of the world.

PART THREE

Precept Recitation Ceremonies

Precept Recitation Ceremonies

1
THREE REFUGES AND TWO PROMISES: RECITATION FOR CHILDREN

Head of Ceremony (chants each of the following four lines, echoed by whole assembly):

> *The Dharma is deep and lovely.*
> *We now have a chance to see it,*
> *study it, and practice it.*
> *We vow to realize its true meaning.*

Head of Ceremony: Today the community has gathered to recite the Three Refuges, the Two Promises, the Five Wonderful Precepts, and the Precepts of the Order of Interbeing. First we will recite the Three Refuges and the Two Promises. Will the younger members of the community please come forward.

Young people, upon hearing the sound of the bell, please bow three times to show your gratitude to the Buddha, the Dharma, and the Sangha.

(bell)

Young students of the Buddha, you have taken refuge in the Buddha, the one who shows you the way in this life; in the Dharma, the way of understanding and love; and in the Sangha, the community that lives in harmony and awareness. It is beneficial to recite the Three Refuges regularly. Will the entire community please join with the young people in repeating after me:

> *I take refuge in the Buddha, the one who shows*
> *me the way in this life.*
> *I take refuge in the Dharma, the way of under-*
> *standing and love.*
> *I take refuge in the Sangha, the community that*
> *lives in harmony and awareness.*

Young students of the Buddha, we have completed the recitation of the Three Refuges. Now we will recite the Two Promises that you have made with the Buddha, the Dharma, and the Sangha. Will the entire community please join the young people in repeating after me:

> *I vow to develop my compassion*
> *In order to love and protect life, the lives of*
> *people, animals, and plants.*

This is the first promise you have made with the Buddha, our teacher. Have you tried to learn more about it and to keep your promise during the past two weeks?

(bell)

> *I vow to develop understanding*
> *In order to love and live in harmony with*
> *people, animals, and plants.*

This is the second promise you have made with the Buddha, our teacher. Have you tried to learn more about it and to keep your promise during the past two weeks?

(bell)

Young students of the Enlightened One, understanding and love are the two most important teachings of the Buddha. If we do not make the effort to be open, to understand the suffering of other people, we will not be able to love them and to live in harmony with them. We should also try to understand and protect the lives of animals and plants and live in harmony with them. If we cannot understand, we cannot love. The Buddha teaches us to look at living beings with the eyes of love and understanding. Please learn to practice this teaching.

Young people, upon hearing the sound of the bell, please bow three times to the Three Jewels, and then you can leave the Meditation Hall.

(three sounds of the bell)

2
RECITING THE FIVE WONDERFUL PRECEPTS

Sangha Karman: Has the entire community assembled?

Reply: The entire community has assembled.

Sangha Karman: Is there harmony in the community?

Reply: Yes, there is harmony.

Sangha Karman: Is there anyone not able to be present who has asked to be represented and have they declared themselves to have done their best to study and practice the precepts?

Reply: No, there is not.

or

Reply: Yes, _____, for health reasons, cannot be at the recitation today. She has asked _____ to represent her and she declares that she has done her best to study and practice the precepts.

Sangha Karman: What is the reason for the community gathering today?

Reply: The community has gathered to practice the recitation of the Five Wonderful Precepts. Noble community, please listen. Today, __(date)__ , has been declared to be the precept recitation day. We have gathered at the appointed time. The noble community is ready to hear and recite the precepts in an atmosphere of harmony, and the recitation can proceed. Is that correct?

Everyone: That is correct.

Head of Ceremony: Brothers and Sisters, it is now time to recite the Five Wonderful Precepts. Please, those who have been ordained as *Upasaka* and *Upasika* kneel with joined palms in the direction of the Buddha, our teacher.

Brothers and Sisters, please listen. The Five Precepts are the basis for a happy life. They have the capacity to protect life and to make it beautiful and worth living. They are also the door that opens to enlightenment and liberation. Please listen to each precept, and answer yes, silently every time you see that you have made the effort to study, practice, and observe it.

THE FIRST PRECEPT

Aware of the suffering caused by the destruction of life, I vow to cultivate compassion and learn ways to protect the lives of people, animals, plants, and minerals. I am determined not to kill, not to let others kill, and not to condone any act of killing in the world, in my thinking, and in my way of life.

(silence)

This is the first of the Five Precepts. Have you made an effort to study and practice it during the past two weeks?

(bell)

THE SECOND PRECEPT

Aware of the suffering caused by exploitation, social injustice, stealing, and oppression, I vow to cultivate loving kindness and learn ways to work for the well-being of people, animals, plants, and minerals. I vow to practice generosity by sharing my time, energy, and material resources with those who are in need. I am determined not to steal and not to possess anything that should belong to others. I will respect the property of others, but I will prevent others from profiting from human suffering or the suffering of other species on Earth.

(silence)

This is the second of the Five Precepts. Have you made an effort to study and practice it during the past two weeks?

(bell)

THE THIRD PRECEPT

Aware of the suffering caused by sexual misconduct, I vow to cultivate responsibility and learn ways to protect the safety and integrity of individuals, couples, families, and society. I am determined not to engage in sexual relations without love and a long-term commitment. To preserve the happiness of myself and others, I am determined to respect my commitments and the commitments of others. I will do everything in my power to protect children from sexual abuse and to prevent couples and families from being broken by sexual misconduct.

(silence)

This is the third of the Five Precepts. Have you made an effort to study and practice it during the past two weeks?

(bell)

THE FOURTH PRECEPT

Aware of the suffering caused by unmindful speech and the inability to listen to others, I vow to cultivate loving speech and deep listening in order to bring joy and happiness to others and relieve others of their suffering. Knowing that words can create happiness or suffering, I vow to learn to speak truthfully, with words that inspire self-confidence, joy, and hope. I am determined not to spread news that I do not know to be certain and not to criticize or condemn things of which I am not sure. I will refrain from uttering words that can cause division or discord, or that can cause the family or the community to break. I will make all efforts to reconcile and resolve all conflicts, however small.

(silence)

This is the fourth of the Five Precepts. Have you made an effort to study and practice it during the past two weeks?

(bell)

THE FIFTH PRECEPT

Aware of the suffering caused by unmindful consumption, I vow to cultivate good health, both physical and mental, for myself, my family, and my society, by practicing mindful eating, drinking, and consuming. I vow to ingest only items that preserve peace, well-being, and joy in my body, in my consciousness, and in the collective body and consciousness of my family and society. I am determined not to use alcohol or any other intoxicant or to ingest foods or other items that contain toxins, such as certain TV programs, magazines, books, films, and conversations. I am aware that to damage my body or my consciousness with these poisons is to betray my ancestors, my parents, my society, and future generations. I will work to transform violence, fear, anger, and confusion in myself and in society by practicing a diet for myself and for society. I understand that a proper diet is crucial for self-transformation and for the transformation of society.

(silence)

This is the fifth of the Five Precepts. Have you made an effort to study and practice it during the past two weeks?

(bell)

Brothers and Sisters, we have recited the Five Wonderful Precepts, the foundation of happiness for the individual, the family, and society. We should recite them regularly so that our study and practice of the precepts can deepen day by day.

Hearing the bell, please bow three times to the Buddha, the Dharma, and the Sangha to show your gratitude.

(three sounds of the bell)

3
RECITING THE FOURTEEN PRECEPTS
OF THE ORDER OF INTERBEING

Sangha Karman: Has the whole community assembled?

Reply: The whole community has assembled.

Sangha Karman: Is there harmony in the community?

Reply: Yes, there is harmony.

Sangha Karman: Is there anyone not able to be present who has asked to be represented and have they declared themselves to have done their best to study and practice the precepts?

Reply: No, there is not.

or

Reply: Yes, Brother (or Sister) True _____ , for health reasons, cannot be at the recitation today. He has asked Brother (or Sister) True _____ to represent him and he declares that he has done his best to study and practice the precepts.

Sangha Karman: What is the reason for the community gathering today?

Reply: The community has gathered to practice the recitation of the Fourteen Precepts of the Order of Interbeing. Noble community, please listen. Today, __(date)_ , has been declared to be the precept recitation day. We have gathered at the appointed time. The noble community is ready to hear and to recite the precepts in an atmosphere of harmony and the recitation can proceed. Is that correct?

Everyone: That is correct.

Head of Ceremony: Today I have been asked by the community to recite the precepts. I ask the community for spiritual support. Please, Brothers and Sisters, listen.

The precepts are the very essence of the Order of Interbeing. They are the torch lighting our path, the boat carrying us, the teacher guiding us. I ask the community to listen with a serene mind. Consider the precepts as a clear mirror in which to look at ourselves. Say yes, silently, every time you see that during the past week you have made an effort to learn, practice, and observe the precept read.

(bell)

Sisters and Brothers, are you ready?

Everyone (silently): I am ready.

These then are the precepts of the Order of Interbeing.

THE FIRST PRECEPT

Do not be idolatrous about or bound to any doctrine, theory, or ideology, even Buddhist ones. Buddhist systems of thought are guiding means; they are not absolute truth.

(silence)

This is the first precept of the Order of Interbeing. Have you studied, practiced, and observed it during the past two weeks?

(bell)

THE SECOND PRECEPT

Do not think the knowledge you presently possess is changeless, absolute truth. Avoid being narrow-minded and bound to present views. Learn and practice nonattachment from views in order to be open to receive others' viewpoints. Truth is found in life and not merely in conceptual knowledge. Be ready to learn throughout your entire life and to observe reality in your-self and in the world at all times.

(silence)

This is the second precept of the Order of Interbeing. Have you studied, practiced, and observed it during the past two weeks?

(bell)

THE THIRD PRECEPT

Do not force others, including children, by any means whatsoever, to adopt your views, whether by authority, threat, money, propaganda, or even education. However, through compassionate dialogue, help others renounce fanaticism and narrowness.

(silence)

This is the third precept of the Order of Interbeing. Have you studied, practiced, and observed it during the past two weeks?

(bell)

THE FOURTH PRECEPT

Do not avoid contact with suffering or close your eyes before suffering. Do not lose awareness of the existence of suffering in the life of the world. Find ways to be with those who are suffering, including personal contact, visits, images, and sounds. By such means, awaken yourself and others to the reality of suffering in the world.

(silence)

This is the fourth precept of the Order of Interbeing. Have you studied, practiced, and observed it during the past two weeks?

(bell)

THE FIFTH PRECEPT

Do not accumulate wealth while millions are hungry. Do not take as the aim of your life fame, profit, wealth, or sensual pleasure. Live simply and share time, energy, and material resources with those who are in need.

(silence)

This is the fifth precept of the Order of Interbeing. Have you studied, practiced, and observed it during the past two weeks?

(bell)

THE SIXTH PRECEPT

Do not maintain anger or hatred. Learn to penetrate and transform them when they are still seeds in your consciousness. As soon as they arise, turn your attention to your breath in order to see and understand the nature of your anger and hatred and the nature of the persons who have caused your anger and hatred.

(silence)

This is the sixth precept of the Order of Interbeing. Have you studied, practiced, and observed it during the past two weeks?

(bell)

THE SEVENTH PRECEPT

Do not lose yourself in dispersion and in your surroundings. Practice mindful breathing to come back to what is happening in the present moment. Be in touch with what is wondrous, refreshing, and healing both inside and around you. Plant seeds of joy, peace, and understanding in yourself in order to facilitate the work of transformation in the depths of your consciousness.

(silence)

This is the seventh precept of the Order of Interbeing. Have you studied, practiced, and observed it during the past two weeks?

(bell)

THE EIGHTH PRECEPT

Do not utter words that can create discord and cause the community to break. Make every effort to reconcile and resolve all conflicts, however small.

(silence)

This is the eighth precept of the Order of Interbeing. Have you studied, practiced, and observed it during the past two weeks?

(bell)

THE NINTH PRECEPT

Do not say untruthful things for the sake of personal interest or to impress people. Do not utter words that cause division and hatred. Do not spread news that you do not know to be certain. Do not criticize or condemn things of which you are not sure. Always speak truthfully and constructively. Have the courage to speak out about situations of injustice, even when doing so may threaten your own safety.

(silence)

This is the ninth precept of the Order of Interbeing. Have you studied, practiced, and observed it during the past two weeks?

(bell)

THE TENTH PRECEPT

Do not use the Buddhist community for personal gain or profit, or transform your community into a political party. A religious community, however, should take a clear stand against oppression and injustice and should strive to change the situation without engaging in partisan conflicts.

(silence)

This is the tenth precept of the Order of Interbeing. Have you studied, practiced, and observed it during the past two weeks?

(bell)

THE ELEVENTH PRECEPT

Do not live with a vocation that is harmful to humans and nature. Do not invest in companies that deprive others of their chance to live. Select a vocation that helps realize your ideal of compassion.

(silence)

This is the eleventh precept of the Order of Interbeing. Have you studied, practiced, and observed it during the past two weeks?

(bell)

THE TWELFTH PRECEPT

Do not kill. Do not let others kill. Find whatever means possible to protect life and prevent war.

(silence)

This is the twelfth precept of the Order of Interbeing. Have you studied, practiced, and observed it during the past two weeks?

(bell)

THE THIRTEENTH PRECEPT

Possess nothing that should belong to others. Respect the property of others, but prevent others from profiting from human suffering or the suffering of other species on Earth.

(silence)

This is the thirteenth precept of the Order of Interbeing. Have you studied, practiced, and observed it during the past two weeks?

(bell)

THE FOURTEENTH PRECEPT

Do not mistreat your body. Learn to handle it with respect. Do not look on your body as only an instrument. Preserve vital energies (sexual, breath, spirit) for the realization of the Way. (For brothers and sisters who are not monks and nuns:) Sexual expression should not take place without love and a long-term commitment. In sexual relationships, be aware of future suffering that may be caused. To preserve the happiness of others, respect the rights and commitments of others. Be fully aware of the responsibility of bringing new lives into the world. Meditate on the world into which you are bringing new beings.

(silence)

This is the fourteenth precept of the Order of Interbeing. Have you studied, practiced, and observed it during the past two weeks?

(bell)

Brothers and Sisters, I have recited the precepts as the community has wished. I thank all my sisters and brothers for helping me do it serenely. Please join your palms and recite each line of the closing chant after me:

> *Reciting the precepts, practicing the way of*
> *awareness*
> *Gives rise to benefits without limit.*
> *I vow to share the fruits with all beings.*
>
> *I vow to offer tribute to parents, teachers,*
> *friends, and numerous beings*
> *Who give guidance and support along the path.*

PART FOUR

The Charter of the Order of Interbeing

The Charter of the Order of Interbeing
(Tiep Hien)

1. A Buddhist community is formed with the name Order of Interbeing.

2. The aim of the Order is to actualize Buddhism by studying, experimenting with, and applying Buddhism in modern life.

3. The Order of Interbeing follows the various traditions of Buddhism in that it has as its base the spirit of nonattachment from views, the spirit of direct experimentation on the nature of interdependent origination through meditation, the spirit of appropriateness, and the spirit of skillful means. All four are to be found in all Buddhist traditions.

4. The Order of Interbeing does not consider any sutra or group of sutras as its basic scripture(s). It draws inspiration from the essence of the Buddhadharma in all sutras. It does not accept the systematic arrangement of the Buddhist teachings proposed by any school. The Order of Interbeing seeks to realize the spirit of the Dharma in early Buddhism, as well as in the development of that spirit through the history of the sangha, and its life and teachings in all Buddhist traditions.

5. The Order of Interbeing considers all sutras, whether spoken by the Lord Buddha or compiled by later Buddhist generations, as Buddhist sutras. It is also able to find inspiration from the texts of other spiritual traditions. It considers the development of original Buddhism into new schools a necessity to keep the spirit of Buddhism alive. Only by proposing new forms of Buddhist life can one help the true Buddhist spirit perpetuate.

6. The life of the Order of Interbeing should be nourished by understanding and compassion. Compassion and understanding, radiated by the Buddhist life, can contribute to the peace and happiness of humankind. The Order considers the principle of nonattachment from views and the principle of direct experimentation on interdependent origination through meditation to be the two most important guides for attaining true understanding. It considers the principle of appropriateness and the principle of skillful means as guides for actions in society. The spirit of nonattachment from views and the spirit of direct experimentation lead to open-mindedness and compassion, both in the realm of the perception of reality and in the realm of human relationships. The spirit of appropriateness and the spirit of skillful means lead to a capacity to be creative and to reconcile, both of which are necessary for the service of living beings.

7. The Order of Interbeing rejects dogmatism in both looking and acting. It seeks all forms of action that can revive and sustain the true spirit of insight and compassion in life. It considers this spirit to be more important than any Buddhist institution or tradition. With the aspiration of a

bodhisattva, members of the Order of Interbeing seek to change themselves in order to change society in the direction of compassion and understanding by living a joyful and mindful life.

CHAPTER III
AUTHORITY, MEMBERSHIP, ORGANIZATION

8. To protect and respect the freedom and responsibility of each member of the community, monks, nuns, and laypeople enjoy equality in the Order of Interbeing.

9. The Order of Interbeing does not recognize the necessity of a mediator between the Buddha and lay disciples, between humans and ultimate reality. It considers, however, the insight and experiences of ancestral teachers, monks, nuns, and laypeople, as helpful to those who are practicing the Way.

10. Members of the Order of Interbeing are either in the Core Community or the Extended Community. The Core Community consists of those who have taken the vow to observe the Fourteen Precepts of the Order and the Five Wonderful Precepts, and who have been ordained as brothers and sisters in the Order. The Extended Community consists of members who, while trying to live up to the spirit of the Order of Interbeing, have not formally taken the vow to observe the Fourteen Precepts, nor received ordination in the Order of Interbeing. The members of the Core Community accept the responsibility to organize and help sustain precept recitations, Days of Mindfulness, and retreats with their local sangha.

11. The Extended Community lives in close relationship with the Core Community by attending the recitation of the precepts every two weeks and by participating in spiritual and social events sponsored by the Core Community.

12. *Dharmacaryas* (Dharma Teachers) are members of the Core Community who have been selected as teachers based on their stability and ability to lead a happy life. They function to inspire joy and stability in the local sanghas. Local sanghas are encouraged to suggest potential Dharmacaryas.

CHAPTER IV

LEADERSHIP, COMMUNITY PROPERTIES, ACCOUNTING

13. Once every two or three years, an assembly of all Core Community members should gather for a council. Members unable to attend can appoint a representative proxy to speak for them. The process of consensus with stand-asides shall be used, and rotating teams of two facilitators, one female, one male, each of different nationality, shall conduct the meeting.

14. At the biannual or triannual meeting, members of the Core Community will select two councils: one of Elder Brothers and Sisters, and one of Younger Brothers and Sisters. The elders will be selected on the basis of life maturity and practice maturity, and the youth on freshness and youth in practice. The councils will form an executive committee to take care of the business of the Order of Interbeing between biannual or triannual assemblies, and will be responsible to the two councils. These two councils will meet together as friends and advise each other.

15. Local sanghas are encouraged to organize in the same way.

16. Any community properties of the Order should be incorporated under the national and local regulations of its site.

17. To protect those who may be responsible for the management of community properties, all assets, including bank accounts, currency, real estate, vehicles, etc., are to be accounted for using common accounting practices. All Order of Interbeing funds, including contributions, are to be held in a bank account under the name "Order of Interbeing." The signatories will be appointed by the Executive Committee of the Council of Elders. A detailed financial report prepared by the Treasurer of the Executive Committee of the Council of Elders shall be presented at the biannual or triannual meeting of the Core Community, and an interim report mailed yearly to each Core Community member.

CHAPTER V
PRECEPTS OF THE ORDER OF INTERBEING,
CONDITIONS FOR ORDINATION

18. The precepts of the Order of Interbeing reflect the life of the Order, which considers spiritual practice as the base of all social action.

19. The precepts are considered the heart of the Charter. Members are expected to recite the Five Wonderful Precepts and the Fourteen Precepts every two weeks. If there is a three-month lapse in their recitation, their ordination is considered nullified.

20. All persons over eighteen years old, regardless of race, nationality, color, gender, or sexual orientation, are eligible to join the Order if they have shown the capacity of learning and practicing the discipline of the Order of Interbeing, and have formally received the Three Refuges and the Five Wonderful Precepts.

21. A candidate shall announce his or her aspiration, in writing, to take the ordination of the Order of Interbeing to the local sangha Core Community members, or if none are located nearby, to the Dharmacaryas. The local sangha Core Community members would then mentor the candidate for at least a year, and when they feel confident that the candidate is happy and steadfast in his or her practice and that he or she practices in harmony with the sangha, the Core Community members will indicate that that candidate is ready to receive ordination in the Order of Interbeing.

22. After the local sangha indicates that the candidate is ready to receive the Order ordination, his or her name is forwarded to the Executive Council. The date and place for ordination will then be decided.

23. Members of the Core Community are expected to observe at least sixty Days of Mindfulness a year. It is recognized that this sixty-day requirement may be difficult for some members to achieve at times due to family or other responsibilities, and the requirement is intended to be flexible in those cases. Members are expected to organize and practice with a sangha.

24. Providing they are consistent with the spirit of the Five Wonderful Precepts and the Fourteen Precepts, all life-styles

(conjugal or celibate) are considered equally valid for Core Community members. The partner of a Core Community member should be a member of the Core Community, or at least a member of the Extended Community.

CHAPTER VI
AMENDMENT OF THE CHARTER

25. Every word and every sentence in this charter is subject to change, so that the spirit of the charter will be allowed to remain alive throughout the history of the practice. Previous versions should be preserved and made available for consultation by later generations.

26. This charter, consisting of six chapters and twenty-eight items should be revised and amended at each biannual or triannual assembly of Core Community members in order to keep it relevant to today's societies.

27. The Fourteen Precepts and the Charter are to be re-examined once every two or three years during the general assembly of Core Community members. All members shall be notified six months in advance of the date and location of the meeting.

28. In keeping with the tradition of the sangha, all changes must be made by consensus and not just by simple majority. The rules of consensus shall be reviewed and revised at the general biannual or triannual assembly.

Parallax Press publishes books and tapes on mindful aware-ness and social responsibility, "making peace right in the moment we are alive." We carry all books and tapes by Thich Nhat Hanh. For a copy of our complete catalog, please write:

Parallax Press
P.O. Box 7355
Berkeley, CA 94707

For further information about the Order of Interbeing, please contact:

Community of Mindful Living
P.O. Box 7355
Berkeley, CA 94707

or

Plum Village
Meyrac
47120 Loubès-Bernac
France